394.261   Schaefer, Lola M.
S   Chinese New Year

PERMA-BOUND   BAR: L0101774

DATE DUE			

$11.95

PENNYCOOK
ELEMENTARY SCHOOL
3620 FERNWOOD DR.
VALLEJO, CA 94591

AR POINTS: 0.5
AR READ LVL: 2.2

Chinese
New Year

by Lola M. Schaefer

Consulting Editor: Gail Saunders-Smith, Ph.D.

Consultant: Xiaohong Shen, Ph.D.
Assistant Director, Center for East Asian Studies
Stanford University

Pebble Books

an imprint of Capstone Press
Mankato, Minnesota

Pebble Books are published by Capstone Press
151 Good Counsel Drive, P.O. Box 669, Mankato, Minnesota 56002
www.capstonepress.com

3 4 5 6 7 8 08 07 06 05 04 03

Library of Congress Cataloging-in-Publication Data
Schaefer, Lola M., 1950–
    Chinese New Year / by Lola M. Schaefer.
    p. cm.—(Holidays and Celebrations)
    Summary: Simple Text and photographs describe and illustrate Chinese New
Year and how it is celebrated.
    ISBN 0-7368-0660-1 (hardcover)
    ISBN 0-7368-9426-X (paperback)
    1. Chinese New Year—Juvenile literature. 2. China—Social life and customs—
Juvenile literature. [1. Chinese New Year. 2. Holidays—China. 3. China—Social life
and customs.] I. Title. II. Series.
GT4905 .S33 2001
394.261—dc21   00-023057

Note to Parents and Teachers

The Holidays and Celebrations series supports national social
studies standards related to culture. This book describes Chinese
New Year and illustrates how it is celebrated. The photographs
support early readers in understanding the text. The repetition of
words and phrases helps early readers learn new words. This book
also introduces early readers to subject-specific vocabulary words,
which are defined in the Words to Know section. Early readers may
need assistance to read some words and to use the Table of
Contents, Words to Know, Read More, Internet Sites, and
Index/Word List sections of the book.

Table of Contents

EMBARCADERO WEST

4

Chinese New Year is the first day of the Chinese Lunar Calendar. This holiday usually takes place during January or February in North America. The celebration lasts for 15 days.

Chinese New Year honors
new beginnings and
the season for planting.
People wish for good luck
in the new year.

People prepare for the Chinese New Year celebration. They clean their homes and get new clothes.

恭賀新禧

恭	喜	發	財
HAPPY NEW YEAR			

People hang words of good luck in their homes. They write them on red paper. The color red stands for good luck in the new year.

Families gather to celebrate New Year's Eve. They eat a special meal.

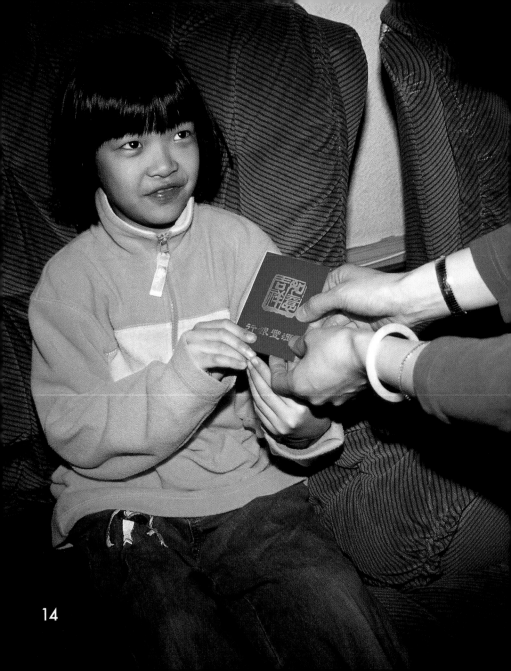

Adults give children gifts of money during Chinese New Year. The money is for good luck.

New Year's Day is a day of kindness and friendship. People bring gifts to their families and friends.

People celebrate the lantern festival on the last day of Chinese New Year. Children light lanterns. They show them to their friends.

Young men dance the lion dance for good luck. Firecrackers and paper dragons end the celebration.

Words to Know

celebrate—to do something fun on a special day; people celebrate Chinese New Year for 15 days.

Chinese Lunar Calendar—a calendar based on the phases of the moon

Chinese New Year—the first day of the Chinese Lunar Calendar; in China, Chinese New Year is celebrated in the spring.

firecrackers—paper tubes filled with gunpowder; firecrackers make a loud noise when they explode; Chinese people believe that firecrackers scare away evil spirits.

lantern—a light with protective sides around it; lanterns can be made out of paper, glass, or metal.

lion dance—a dance that Chinese people believe brings good luck to homes or businesses

Demi. *Happy, Happy Chinese New Year.* New York: Crown Publishers, 2003.

Flanagan, Alice K. *Chinese New Year.* Holidays and Festivals. Minneapolis: Compass Point Books, 2004.

Robinson, Fay. *Chinese New Year—A Time for Parades, Family, and Friends.* Finding out about Holidays. Berkeley Heights, N.J.: Enslow, 2001.

Internet Sites

FactHound offers a safe, fun way to find Internet sites related to this book. All of the sites on FactHound have been researched by our staff.
Here's how:

1. Visit *www.facthound.com.*
2. Type in this special code **0736806601** for age-appropriate sites. Or enter a search word related to this book for a more general search.
3. Click on the **Fetch It** button.

FactHound will fetch the best sites for you!

Index/Word List

Word Count: 176
Early-Intervention Level: 14

Editorial Credits
Mari C. Schuh, editor; Heather Kindseth, designer; Kimberly Danger and
  Heidi Schoof, photo researchers

Photo Credits
David F. Clobes, 8, 16
Lawrence Migdale, 12
Brain Cyr, cover
John Elk III, 1, 4, 18
Patrick Batchelder, 6
Trip/H. Rogers, 10; P. Kwan, 14; R. Nichols, 20